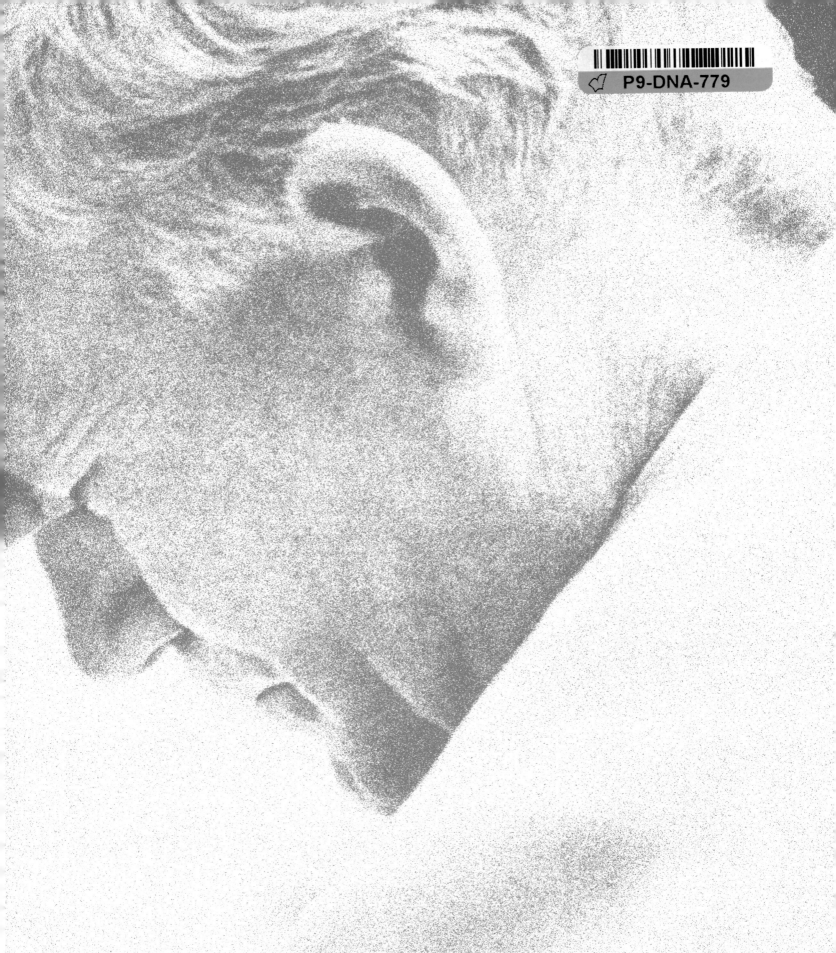

AS
PASTOR
AND
BROTHER

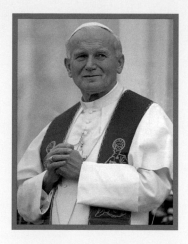

IN MEMORY OF
POPE JOHN PAUL II'S
VISITS TO CANADA

A CANWEST BOOK
A subsidiary of CanWest Global Communications

Published by CanWest Books Inc.
A subsidiary of CanWest Global Communications
1450 Don Mills Road
Toronto, ON
Canada, M3B 2X7

National Library of Canada Cataloguing in Publication Data

McAuley, Lynn, 1956
AS PASTOR AND BROTHER
In Memory of Pope John Paul II's Visits to Canada
Editor Lynn McAuley
Journalist: CanWest Newspaper journalists
PhotoJournalist: CanWest Newspaper photojournalists

ISBN 0-9737410-2-3

Pages 128 constitutes a continuation of the copyright page

Jacket and text design by Gordon Sibley
Prepress Emerson Group
Cover photograph: AP Photo/Plinio Lepri
Printed and bound in Canada by Friesens

First Edition

10 9 8 7 6 5 4 3 2 1

CONTENTS

FOREWORD

Pope John Paul II was sought out by so many millions in so many lands. But what did he go out to see?

He went abroad, and came to Canada, as a pilgrim. A pilgrim is one who seeks to find the traces of the divine in this world.

There is natural geography – the wonders of the mountains and the seacoast, of rivers and lakes and waterfalls.

And there are historical places – political capitals, trading posts, centres of commerce, battlefields.

But overlaying all of this is the work of Providence in the world, a sort of divine itinerary which the finger of God has designated as holy. Places that would otherwise be overlooked: Bethlehem, Assisi, Guadalupe, and yes, Ste-Anne-de-Beaupre, or University Avenue in Toronto during World Youth Day 2002.

The pilgrim goes in search of such places. So too did John Paul II, going to the ends of the earth to see the mighty works of God. The mightiest of all those works is the human person – the person created in the image of God and redeemed by His Son. Every human life was a question, John Paul believed, to which Jesus Christ was the answer.

That's why he came to Canada. To seek out the face of God in the modern world, and to proclaim salvation to all of us who live here.

And when he came, we too glimpsed in him something of the mighty works of God.

— *Father Raymond J. de Souza*

AS PASTOR AND BROTHER

BY RANDY BOSWELL

There's a snapshot on top of Jack Parsons' piano that has a place of pride among his most cherished belongings. The twenty-year-old photograph of his infant daughter, Jennifer, being kissed by Pope John Paul II is no mere memento; faith and wonder have transformed it into a kind of religious relic, an object imbued with real spiritual power for a Newfoundland family with deep Catholic roots.

On September 12, 1984, the Pope came to the village of Flat Rock, near St. John's, to see a windswept grotto — a tribute to the Virgin Mary built by devout islanders in the nineteenth century — and bless the fishing boats that ply the waters off Canada's East Coast. It was a brief stop in the town of 950 souls, but the visit by the 263rd successor to St. Peter, Christianity's most famous fisherman, left a deep and lasting impression.

"It was the first time he'd been to North America, and he came here," says Parsons, still sounding surprised and moved two decades after the papal pilgrimage to his hometown.

"It was pretty exciting that whole day," he recalls. "We went out to greet the Pope. You could see him coming down the road. Our daughter was only a year old or so. And I was holding her in my arms as he was walking up through the crowd to say a few prayers at the grotto. He reached his hands out and pulled her into him. He kissed her. And my brother snapped a little picture."

That image, he says, and the experience of meeting the Pope face to face, created a shining memory for the entire Parsons clan, strengthening his family's connection to the church.

"That was a big thing that day, and it's stayed with us as a family," he says. "Right from the time you were born, you were Catholic. But it was more of a spiritual thing seeing him that day. Prior to that, yes, he was the head of the church, but all you ever did was read about him or see pictures. Now all of a sudden here was this person, for real. It's a mystical type of thing, you know? You've touched Jesus' representative on Earth."

During his time as pope, John Paul came to see Canada and its eleven million Roman Catholics three times — in 1984, 1987 and 2002 — for a total of twenty-one days. The stays were brief, but like the fleeting encounter that helped nourish the Parsons family's faith, the papal visits are woven into the fabric of the communities he toured, and into the history of the country, leaving an indelible imprint on countless lives.

The man who would become pope had also been to Canada in 1969, when he was still a relatively obscure young cardinal from Poland named Karol Wojtyla. But his papal tours would draw enormous attention and millions of witnesses.

The moment captured in the Parsons' coveted photo was like hundreds of other moments during the Pope's Canadian visits, a steady accumulation of handshakes and blessings, kisses and smiles. But there were also stern warnings against abortion, materialism, euthanasia and pre-marital sex from a determinedly conservative pontiff. And there were provocative, sometimes controversial, pronouncements about aboriginal alienation, unemployment, the eighteenth-century mistreatment of Acadians and other festering wounds in Canadian society.

"Despite the trials of deportation and even the threat of annihilation because of political vicissitudes, the Acadians remained faithful to their faith, faithful to their culture, faithful to their land," the Pope said during a 1984 stop in Moncton, New Brunswick.

The 1984 tour — a gruelling, twelve-day, coast-to-coast odyssey that came at perhaps the height of the Pope's global ministry — stands apart for its scope and significance. It was, in fact, the first time a serving pope had set foot on Canadian soil.

And it was at Quebec City, the very place where Christianity took root in Canada during the age of New France, where John Paul poignantly kissed the ground upon his historic arrival in the country.

"It is in the city of Quebec that the Bishop of Rome sets foot on this land for the first time," the Pope said later that day during a homily at Laval University. "Here began the evangelization of Canada. Here was founded its church. Here was the first diocese of North America. It is from here that the seed first sown began its immense growth."

The visit came at a time when church teachings about birth control and divorce were being challenged by rapidly shifting social attitudes. The sense that the Pope was arriving in Canada during an era of difficult adjustment and sweeping change was reinforced by the fact that he was greeted at the start of his tour in Quebec City by Liberal prime minister John Turner and escorted upon his departure from Ottawa's airport by newly elected Conservative prime minister Brian Mulroney, sworn in just days before.

"In the next eleven days I shall cross your country from one ocean to the other," the Pope said at the start of his tour. "I have some questions to ask you and I would like also to hear yours. I would like to speak to you about the issues of our times concerning culture, the community, technology, the family, sharing and justice. I wish, above all, to speak to you about the fundamental problems — about the faith, about the experience of God, about hope."

The Pope had come, he humbly declared, "as pastor and brother" of the Canadian Catholic community, and more broadly of the people of a nation with a richly layered Christian heritage.

But the humble pontiff moved about the country with the pull of a rock star, drawing crowds of 350,000 to an outdoor mass at Montreal's Jarry Park, 100,000 at Moncton's Magnetic Hill, 200,000 in Winnipeg, 150,000 in rural Alberta, 200,000 in Abbotsford, British Columbia, at least 400,000 in Ottawa and more than 500,000 at Downsview Airport in Toronto — at the time the largest throng of Canadians that had ever gathered in one place.

There was a special meeting, too, with 60,000 Canadians and Americans of Polish descent at Toronto's Exhibition Stadium, where the Pope spotted a Solidarity banner and dramatically veered from his prepared statement to voice support for the then-outlawed Polish trade union.

Throughout his travels, unforgettable images of the Pope were emblazoned into the nation's memory. He was transported everywhere in a cleverly refitted pickup truck dubbed "the Popemobile," a Canadian-made contraption that had a glass bubble to protect the pontiff from a possible repeat of the 1981 assassination attempt that had nearly killed him.

He joined a circle of buckskin-clad native children at Ste-Marie-Among-the-Hurons, the historic reconstruction of an Ontario camp where Christian missionaries were martyred in the seventeenth century. He said mass under a soaring, dove-like canopy in a sun-drenched farmer's field near Edmonton. He rode a specially constructed papal barge along the Rideau Canal in Ottawa before leading his final service of the tour in an open field in the shadow of Parliament Hill.

The Pope, clearly touched by the adulation shown in the enormous numbers drawn to his appearances, was nevertheless careful to urge worshippers to keep seeking Christ after the frenzy had abated, after the crowds had dispersed, after the papal delegation had moved on.

"My word," John Paul said, "does not claim to furnish an answer to all your questions or to replace your searching. But it will offer you the light and strength of faith in Jesus Christ."

Remarkably, the one thing that didn't go right in 1984 turned out to be a wondrous blessing. Despite two attempts, thick fog prevented the Pope's plane from landing for a scheduled visit in Fort Simpson, a remote native community in the Northwest Territories.

The missed meeting, a heartbreaker for thousands of Catholic Dene and other northerners who had travelled to see John Paul, set the stage for a risky papal promise: one day, the Pope said, he would find a way to visit the community.

Three years later, at the end of a hugely successful ten-day tour of the United States, the Pope fulfilled his pledge to the little town on the banks of the Mackenzie River. After an overnight stop in Edmonton, he flew in for a whirlwind visit that attracted about 3,000 people — one of the smallest crowds he would ever address, but which made for a uniquely intimate gathering of the faithful.

Under a stunning rainbow, emblematic to all Christians of a solemn promise kept, the Pope met with tribal elders inside a giant teepee that had been preserved as an altar platform since the papal postponement three years earlier.

And as he had during his 1984 visit to Canada, John Paul weighed carefully — but pointedly — into the politics of the day, this time on the question of aboriginal self-government.

With Canada and its provinces set to embark on a new round of constitutional negotiations, he urged his listeners to pursue a "new covenant to ensure your basic aboriginal rights.

"Today, I pray that the Holy Spirit will help you all to find the just way so that Canada may be a model for the world in upholding the dignity of the aboriginal peoples," he said.

"The soul of the native peoples of Canada is hungry for the spirit of God — because it is hungry for justice, peace, love, goodness, fortitude, responsibility and human dignity," John Paul added. "This is a decisive time in your history. It is essential that you be spiritually strong and clear-sighted as you build the future of your tribes and nations. Be assured that the church will walk that path with you."

While the Pope's pronouncement was addressed broadly to the country's First Nations, his words and presence were most keenly felt by those who had gathered with him that day in Fort Simpson.

"It was an awesome something," remembers eighty-four-year-old Evalie Murdock, who had travelled twenty hours by bus from northern B.C. to meet the man she reverently calls "the Vicar of Christ."

She was perfectly positioned for a personal greeting, and as the Pope made his way past the crowd, she reached out and was rewarded for her pilgrimage.

"We shook hands with him," she says. "I still think about it. To me, it was like I was meeting the Lord Jesus Himself."

Nearly fifteen years would pass before the Pope's next, and last, visit to Canada. By the time he arrived in Toronto in July 2002 to play host to some 200,000 pilgrims attending World Youth Day festivities, he was an alert but increasingly frail octogenarian. John Paul's advancing arthritis and Parkinson's disease had fuelled speculation that his travelling days would soon be over, and that all of his Toronto appearances would be made in a wheelchair.

On the morning the Pope's plane was to touch down in Canada, sixteen-year-old Anthony Ramuscak rose at 5:30 a.m. and hauled himself into his own wheelchair. Paralysed since a 1995 stroke, the devoutly Catholic teen from Hamilton, Ontario, had written letters for months hoping to win a chance to meet John Paul. His prayers, quite literally, were answered just days before World Youth Day was to begin.

Anthony's mother, Rose, a Croatian-born cleaning woman, said her son had always dreamed of becoming a priest, even after the stroke had slurred his speech and left him severely disabled.

Meeting the Pope would only deepen the desire, she believed, and she had made "many, many" phone calls pleading for Anthony to be given a chance during the Toronto visit.

"It was his wish, even since he was a little child, he always wanted to go to Rome," she says. "I said to him, 'Anthony, I would have to win the 6/49.' I'm a single mother. Who has that kind of money to go?

"When we heard the Pope was coming to Toronto, he started sending the letters. And every letter came back saying, 'Anthony, we are sorry, we cannot grant you that wish.' He was nearly heartbroken. Then the phone call came."

Anthony was chosen to be among a select group of Catholic youth to greet John Paul at the Toronto airport. Mother and son were there hours ahead of time, and witnessed the Pope's surprising descent down the aircraft steps rather than a specially made lift.

"The pontiff is old and weak," Anthony recalls in a written account of his experience that day. "Yet he walked down those stairs. That, my dear friends, is a sign: 'If I can do it, so can you.'"

Upon his arrival, the Pope recalled his earlier trips to Canada and voiced his regret that this visit would not include travels throughout the country.

"Dear people of Canada, I have vivid memories of my first apostolic visit in 1984, and of my brief visit in 1987 to the First Nations in the land of Denendeh," he said on July 23, 2002. "This time I must be content to stay only in Toronto. From here I greet all Canadians. You are in my thankful prayers to God, who has so abundantly blessed your vast and beautiful country."

But this peaceable and bountiful nation, the Pope went on to say, was not only a gift from God but also a product of its people's devotion to Christian values.

"Canadians are heirs to an extraordinarily rich humanism, enriched even more by the blend of many different cultural elements," he said. "But the core of your heritage is the spiritual and transcendent vision of life based on Christian revelation which gave vital impetus to your development as a free, democratic and caring society, recognized throughout the world as a champion of human rights and human dignity."

Then came the meeting Anthony had sought for years. He was wheeled to centre stage. And when the Pope raised his hand to perform a blessing, the young man began to sob.

"When I met the pontiff face to face, and I spoke those words to him — 'Blessed be Jesus and Mary' in my Croatian language — it was amazing. I could not help but to burst into tears."

Cameras everywhere flashed. The encounter would produce perhaps the single most memorable image of the 2002 papal visit, and one of the most touching of his three trips to Canada.

Anthony's resolve to become a priest has dramatically strengthened, his mother says. He has gained the will to reduce his weight — "forty or fifty pounds so far," she says — and thus lessen the most serious threat to his health.

His life, adds Rose, which was once sharply divided into the years preceding and following his stroke, is now discussed in terms of "before and after the blessing."

"That moment," says Anthony, "will be with me forever."

Yet there were other enduring moments during the Pope's final visit to Canada. One was the day when more than 100,000 of the young Catholics attending World Youth Day poured onto University Avenue in downtown Toronto to recreate the Way of the Cross — Christ's sorrowful procession through the streets of Jerusalem on His way to be crucified.

The Pope was so moved by the ceremony that he summoned several of the event's leaders to personally thank them for their act of devotion.

John Paul, often appearing older than his eighty-two years because of his health troubles, took a brief and rare respite during his 2002 visit to Canada. He spent four days at a religious retreat on Strawberry Island in cottage country north of Toronto, and even enjoyed a boat tour on Lake Simcoe during his short holiday.

But there was still difficult business to attend to before the Pope's final day in Canada, Monday, July 29, 2002. The day before, at a service in Toronto attended by some 800,000 people — easily surpassing the record-setting crowd he'd drawn in the same city eighteen years earlier — John Paul confronted the most troubling issue facing the church at that time: the sexual abuse of children by a number of Roman Catholic priests across North America.

Acknowledging the "sins and failings" of those members of the clergy, the Pope expressed his "deep sense of sadness and shame.

"But think of the vast majority of dedicated and generous priests," he added, "whose only wish is to serve and do good."

One of the last wishes John Paul expressed before his final departure from Canada was that young Christians in this country and around the world commit themselves to restoring faith in humanity and "building the city of God within the city of man."

In an era marked by terrorism and ethnic and religious strife, he said, the world's youth had a special mission to create a better world.

"The future is in your hearts and in your hands," the Pope said in one of his last Canadian appearances. "God is entrusting to you the task, at once difficult and uplifting, of working with him in the building of the civilization of love."

Quebec City, Quebec ~ September 9-20,

1984

He came, he told us, as a pastor and brother,

full of compassion, gentleness and humour. Pope John Paul II

came, too, with resolve to bring comfort to Canada's

eleven million Roman Catholics at a time when their church was

troubled. He set the tone for his twelve-day cross-country visit in

Quebec, his first stop, where in his eight addresses, he touched

on such issues as maintaining faith and spirituality in a material

world, the vocation of priests, the status of women in the church,

abortion, aboriginal rights and divorce.

John Paul II spoke to the people of Quebec, where more than half of the country's Roman Catholics lived, even before he landed in Canada, addressing them over the radio from his plane as it flew over the Gaspé: "Here, 450 years ago, Jacques Cartier raised the cross. Here, in the presence of the first inhabitants of this land, he knelt together with his men to venerate the standard of our salvation. Here, they opened a new chapter in the history of the world and of the church."

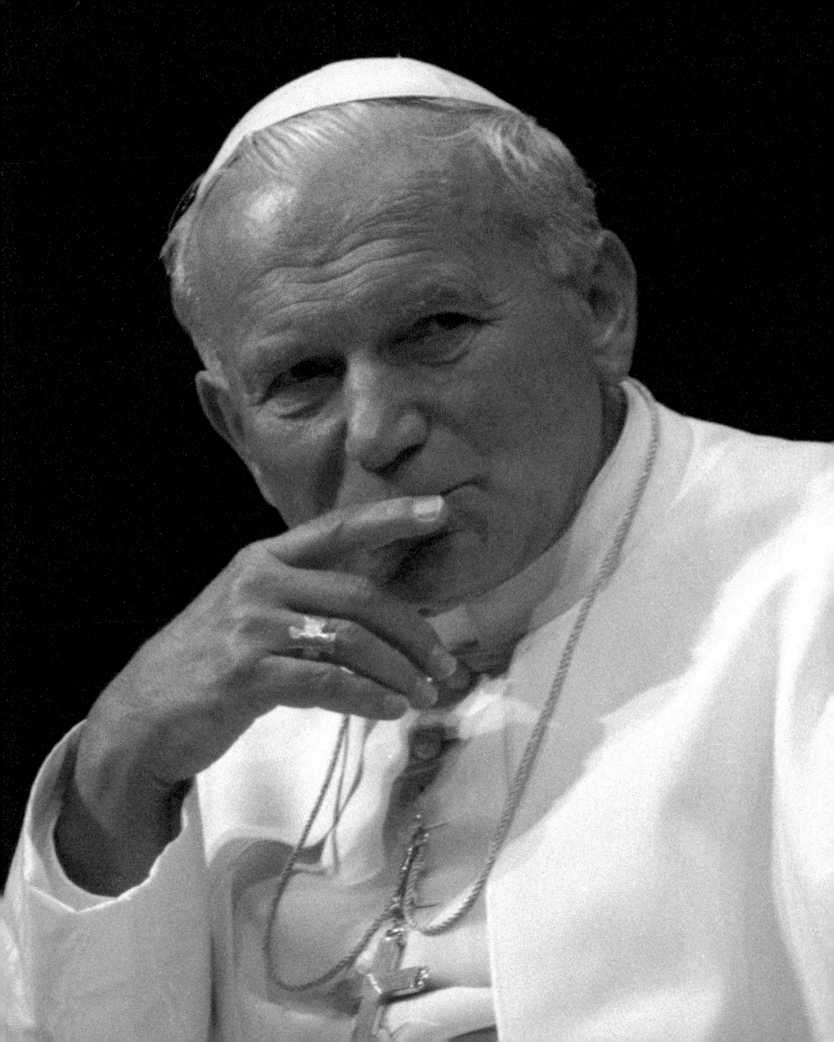

STE-FOY
AIRPORT,
QUEBEC CITY,
QUEBEC
SUNDAY,
SEPTEMBER 9

Pope John Paul II arrived at Quebec City's Ste-Foy airport just before noon in the fading warmth of a late summer sun. As he had on other journeys — and as he would again — he stooped to kneel and kiss the ground, only to be startled by the first round of a twenty-one gun salute. He jumped to his feet.

The Pope arrived in an Alitalia DC 10 flying both the Canadian flag and the papal flag. The plane had been christened the *Luigi Pirandello*.

"I would like to speak to you about the issues of our times concerning culture, the community, technology, the family, sharing and justice…. I wish, above all, to speak to you about the fundamental problems: about the faith, about the experience of God, about hope. My word does not claim to furnish an answer to your questions or to replace your searching. But it will offer you the light and the strength of faith in Jesus Christ as proclaimed by Peter himself in Galilee: 'You are the Christ, Son of the living God'."

— Excerpt from Pope John Paul II's speech at Ste-Foy airport, Quebec City

He was greeted by Governor-General Jeanne Sauvé, who hailed him as a "prophet," soon-to-be former Prime Minister John Turner and his wife, Geills, and Quebec premier Rene Lévèsque

" May my pilgrimage here be the symbol of your journey in the faith.**"**

— Excerpt from Pope John Paul II's greetings to Canadians

For his trek through the streets of Old Quebec City, Pope John Paul II boarded a Canadian-made Popemobile. Air-conditioned and protected by bullet-proof glass, two Popemobiles would leap-frog across the country in Canadian Armed Forces Hercules helicopters, allowing the crowds that lined the streets during every stop to see the pontiff as he passed. Both Popemobiles were modeled on vehicles introduced for European tours after an attempt on the Pope's life in 1981.

Thousands lined the streets as the pontiff passed, cheering and waving the ubiquitous yellow-and-white papal flags and pennants that were among the hundreds of souvenirs being sold. Many others held up home-made banners and signs greeting the Pope or seeking his blessings.

NOTRE DAME DE QUEBEC CATHEDRAL, QUEBEC CITY, QUEBEC

After receiving the key to the city from Mayor Jean Pelletier, the pontiff visited the Quebec City cathedral and the tomb of the first bishop in Canada, François de Laval, whom he had beatified in 1980. The chapel was filled with representatives of the earliest religious orders of New France, including Franciscans and Capuchins friars, Jesuit priests and Ursuline sisters.

LAVAL UNIVERSITY, QUEBEC CITY, QUEBEC

An estimated crowd of 300,000 congregated at Laval University Stadium where Pope John Paul II celebrated mass. Many in the crowd had travelled long distances across the province and many more arrived before dawn. They would spend twelve hours under a blazing sun, lining up for refreshments and toilets, jockeying for places to watch the mass. While it had all the makings of a Sunday picnic, the crowd managed to keep a solemn vigil.

This was a diverse crowd. Teenagers in shorts and tank tops stood beside nuns in full habit. Vendors strolled through the crowd selling buttons, Bibles, flags and papal roses. By the time the Pope arrived at five o'clock, the heat of the day had yielded to a cool evening.

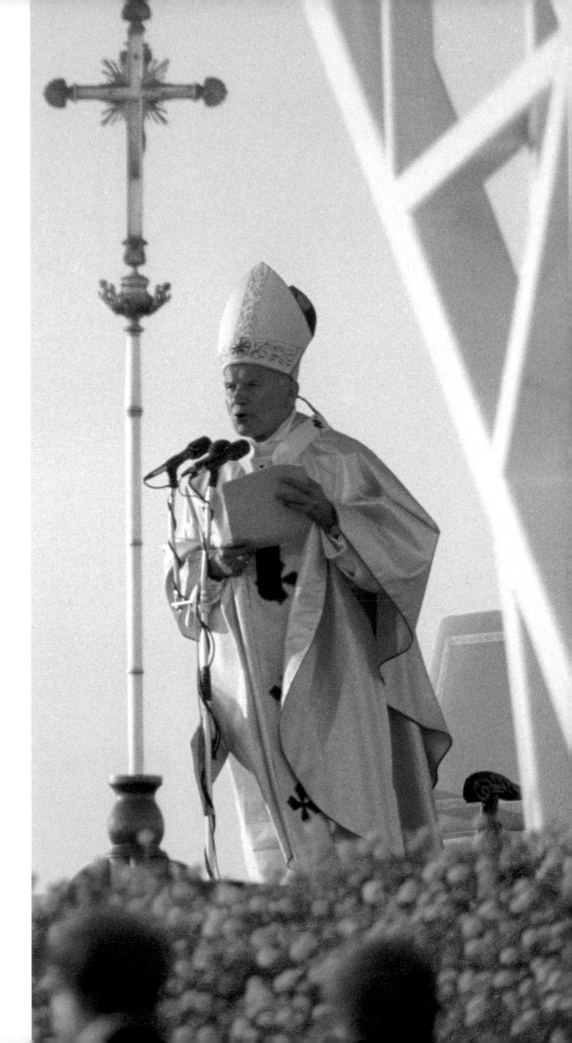

The Pope celebrated the mass from an impressive altar that had been elevated into the stadium's bowl so that even those on the crest of a faraway hill could see and hear the pontiff. The altar was bedecked in red and gold marigolds and on a stage nearby 500 priests, wearing gold-and-white robes, stood guard. Four giant television screens ensured the mass could be seen from anywhere in the stadium

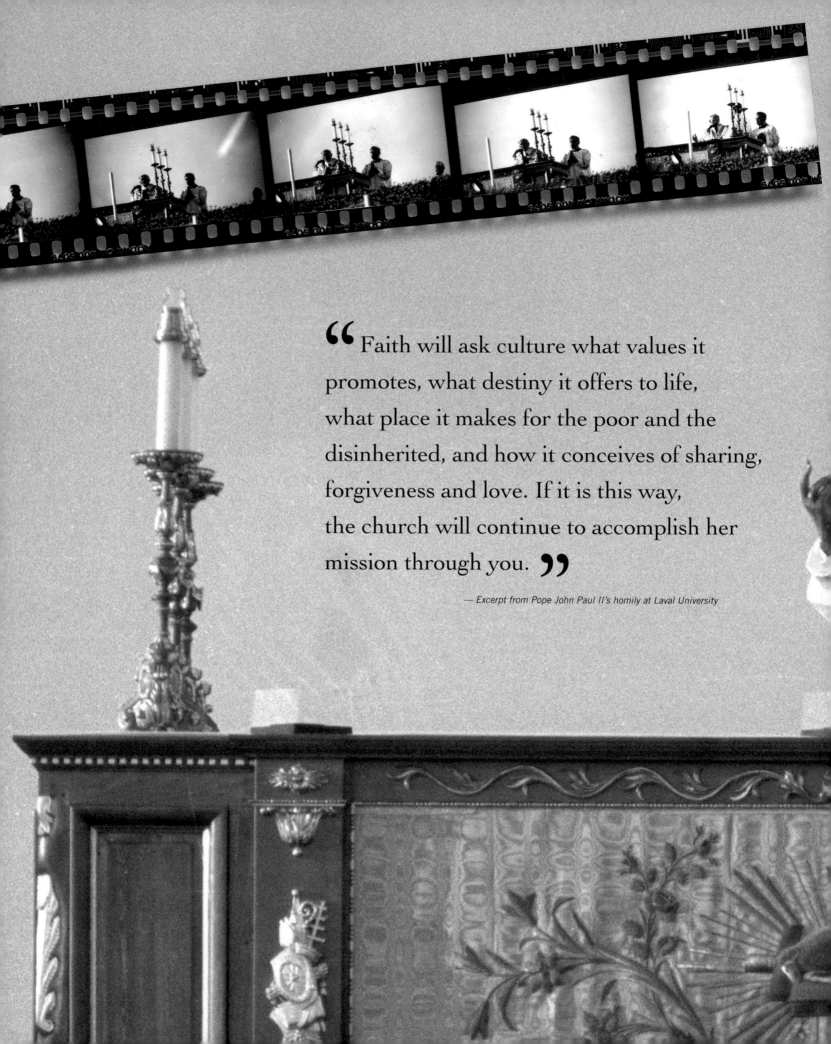

"Faith will ask culture what values it promotes, what destiny it offers to life, what place it makes for the poor and the disinherited, and how it conceives of sharing, forgiveness and love. If it is this way, the church will continue to accomplish her mission through you."

— *Excerpt from Pope John Paul II's homily at Laval University*

STE-ANNE-DE-BEAUPRÉ, QUEBEC, MONDAY, SEPTEMBER 10

The Pope met native leaders from all over Quebec and the Maritimes. On the steps of the famous basilica at Ste-Anne-de-Beaupré, the pontiff was surrounded by bishops in their magenta skullcaps and sashes and chiefs representing nine Indian and Inuit bands. In a passionate, strongly worded address, he told native Canadians to be the "architects of your own future, freely and responsibly … In many places, the native people are among the poorest and most marginal members of society. They suffer from the fact that recognition of their identity and of their ability to participate in shaping their future is late in coming."

CAP DE LA MADELEINE, QUEBEC

The theme of the visit to Cap de la Madeleine was devotion to the Blessed Virgin Mary. Throughout his papacy, Pope John Paul II strove to emphasize Mary's role in Catholic piety and in front of the crowd of about 90,000, who had persisted through a steady downpour, he praised the humility and unfailing faith of the woman who first believed Jesus was the Son of God.

ST. JOSEPH'S ORATORY, MONTREAL, QUEBEC, TUESDAY, SEPTEMBER 11

On his third day in Canada, the pontiff visited St. Joseph's Oratory, a world-famous shrine for Catholic pilgrims. There, he addressed 3,000 white-robed priests, telling them to resist the winds of change.

“ The more a society becomes dechristianized, the more it is touched by uncertainty and indifference, the more it needs to find in the person of priests that radical faith which is like a beacon in the night or a rock on which it can stand. ”

— *Excerpt from Pope John Paul II's address to the clergy*

JARRY PARK, MONTREAL, QUEBEC

The Pope wended his way through the streets of Montreal in the Popemobile, greeted and cheered by crowds along his route to Jarry Park. At the stadium, he celebrated an outdoor mass attended by 350,000 and beatified Sister Marie-Léonie Paradis, founder of the Little Sisters of the Holy Family, moving her one step closer to sainthood.

NOTRE DAME BASILICA, MONTREAL, QUEBEC

At Notre Dame Basilica in downtown Montreal, the pontiff was greeted by 2,500 school children who chanted and sang, giggling as the Pope waded through the crowd, accepting small gifts and whispering confidences that moved those chosen to tears.

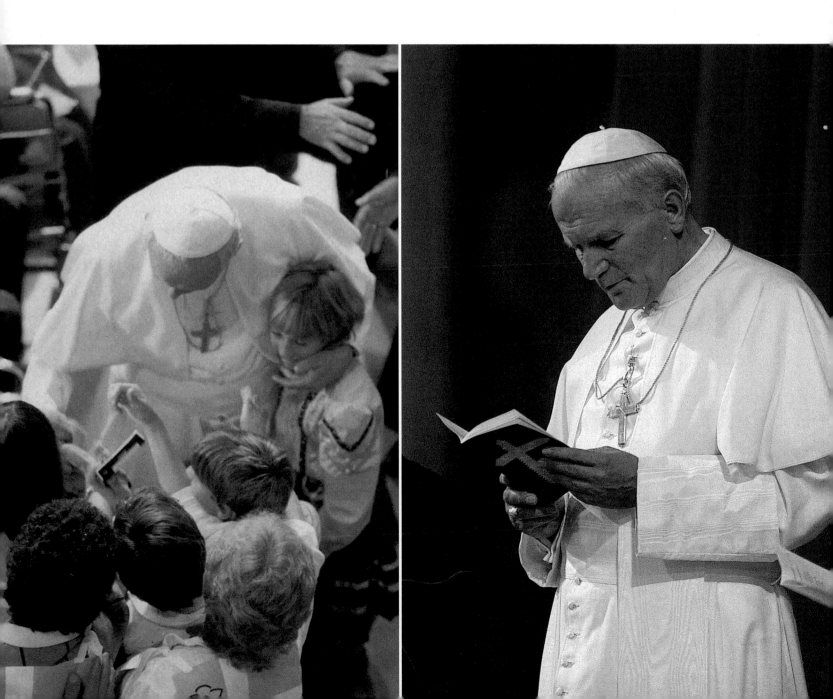

OLYMPIC STADIUM, MONTREAL, QUEBEC

Pope John Paul II's relationship with young people was special and treasured by both. On his last day in Montreal, he attended a youth rally at Olympic Stadium. The crowd was inspired and enthusiastic, waving special white scarves and eager to celebrate.

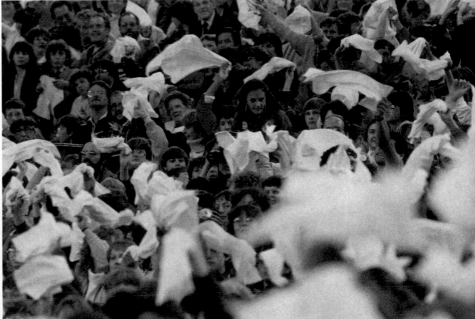

By the end of Pope John Paul II's visit to Quebec, the tenor for this first Canadian visit had been set. For three days, the people of Quebec had had the pontiff as their pastor. They had felt his palpable passion to protect the traditions and faith of the Catholic Church in an increasingly secular society, to preserve human dignity and to pursue justice for the disadvantaged. But, they, like many Canadians to follow, had been touched by the man: his humour, his kindness, his appeal to young and old.

FLAT ROCK, NEWFOUNDLAND, WEDNESDAY, SEPTEMBER 12

This visit to a tiny east-shore fishing village, population 950, was specially chosen for the Pope, who follows in the footsteps of St. Peter, the first pope and a fisherman. A full five hours before the pontiff arrived, a fleet of thirty fishing boats had formed a cross in the sea, bobbing in the deep blue water of the harbour, buffeted by a stiff wind. If the crowd of 3,000 in any way disappointed him (organizers had expected 20,000), the Pope did not show it. He smiled, waved and offered a blessing to the fleet: "I greet you and your family by your ship radio. Through you, I greet all who are on the sea. May I wish you a good fishery, safe passage and God's blessing."

Sitting on the grass-covered rock, hundreds huddled beside the altar, hoping the forecasted rain would bypass the village. It didn't. Almost as soon as the Popemobile drew to a stop and the Salvation Army band struck up *Star of the Sea*, the skies opened with a steady rain. But it did not dampen the Pope's passion as he spoke on a favourite theme — championing human dignity.

MEMORIAL UNIVERSITY,
ST. JOHN'S, NEWFOUNDLAND

An enthusiastic crowd of 3,000 — organizers blamed overzealous security for the poor turnout throughout the province — greeted the Pope at this outdoor rally. Despite the downpour, they roared so loudly when he entered the stadium that the pontiff playfully covered his ears. The good humour prevailed as a dance troupe suddenly broke into *Singin in the Rain* while the Pope tapped his toes in time with the music. He was presented with a white, embroidered parka, trimmed with white fox fur and made by the women of St. Anthony, Newfoundland.

MONCTON, NEW BRUNSWICK, THURSDAY, SEPTEMBER 13

Pope John Paul II spent seven hours in New Brunswick en route to Halifax, making stops at the Notre Dame de l'Assomption Cathedral and Magnetic Hill. The rain and dreary skies that had marked his trip to Newfoundland followed him here. At the cathedral, the pontiff addressed 1,500 descendents of the Acadians, the first Roman Catholics in the area, praising their ancestors as a people who had overcome persecution for their faith and culture. Before his speech, he spoke to five ordinary Canadians — a doctor, a teacher, a nun, a homemaker and a policeman — the first time on this trip ordinary Canadians had an opportunity to speak with the Pope.

MAGNETIC HILL, MONCTON, NEW BRUNSWICK

During the mass on Magnetic Hill, which was attended by more than 100,000, the Pope celebrated the Eucharist with the gold chalice given to Acadian priest Rev. Francois-Michel Richard by Pope Pius X. Father Richard, a key figure in Acadian culture during the late 1800s, had appealed to Pope Pius to name a bishop for Acadians.

"I am very pleased with meeting so many young people. I am very, very pleased and I thank you from all my heart."

— *Pope John Paul II's addresses the youth rally at The Commons, Halifax, Nova Scotia, Thursday, September 13*

HALIFAX, NOVA SCOTIA

The Holy Father began his visit in Halifax by celebrating the Catholic faith at a youth rally at the Central Commons. Friday morning he stopped at Izaak Walton Killam hospital to bless fifty ailing children and their parents, where he reminded the staff of "the special love which Jesus has for the handicapped and the sick, for children and all who suffer." He returned to the Central Commons for an outdoor mass attended by 120,000 and celebrated at an altar set before seven large sails, symbolizing the sea-faring history of the Maritimes.

Pope John Paul II's arrival in
Toronto surprised organizers who
were overwhelmed by the large
emotional crowds, culminating in
the mass of half-a-million faithful
at Canadian Armed Forces Base
Downsview — the largest throng of
Canadians ever gathered in one
spot. Security was especially tight
in Toronto where police received
more than 120 death threats on
the Pope's life. The security
operation for the Canadian papal
visit was the biggest ever mounted
in the country.

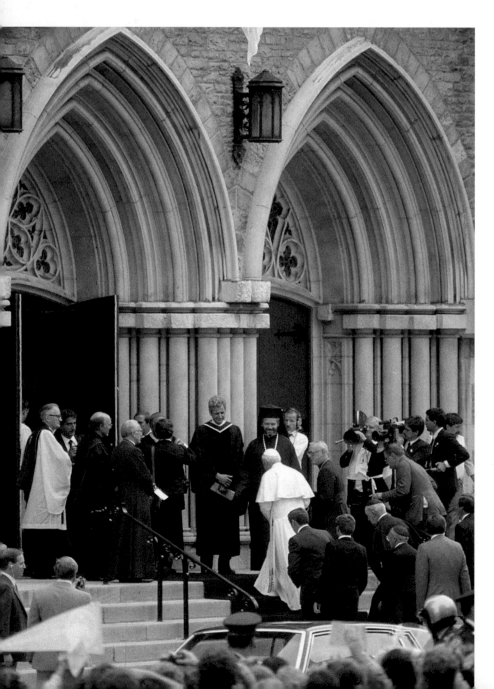

After stopping at Nathan Philips' Square to light the peace flame, the Pope spoke to 1,500 representatives of thirty-five Christian churches at the first ecumenical service at St. Paul's Anglican Church in downtown Toronto. He pledged support of the "complete unity of Christians" saying it is of "crucial importance for the evangelization of the world."

During a frequently emotional address to a Polish rally of 60,000 at Toronto's Canadian National Exhibition Stadium, he praised Solidarity, the Polish trade union which spearheaded the downfall of communism in Eastern Europe, for highlighting the cause of human dignity. Throughout the rally, the crowd, which cheered and waved banners with slogans such as "Lead Us Through Love to Independence," met the Pope's obvious emotion with an enthusiasm of their own. "I see a sign that says Scouts Love the Holy Father," joked the Pope. "Well, the Holy Father loves the Scouts."

MIDLAND, ONTARIO,
SATURDAY, SEPTEMBER 15

After the whirlwind trip through Toronto, Pope John Paul II left to celebrate faith steeped in tradition and history by addressing an assembly of 80,000 at the Shrine of the Canadian Martyrs, the eight Jesuit priests and their helpers who were killed in the seventeenth century. In an earlier ceremony at Ste. Marie Among the Hurons, he watched as members of the local native community performed their own religious ceremony, presenting the pontiff with an eagle feather, a symbol of knowledge.

Despite chilling winds and
near-zero temperatures,
worshippers from as far away as
Texas gathered early and waited
through the day, cheering when
the pontiff arrived and departed
aboard an army-green Canadian
Forces helicopter.

CANADIAN ARMED FORCES BASE DOWNSVIEW, TORONTO

The unseasonably cold and windy September day did not dampen the spirits of the more than half-a-million people who thronged to the armed forces base in Toronto's west end (previous page). An overnight downpour had left the field thick with mud and forced many to abandon their sodden tents for higher ground. When a burst of fireworks signalled the Pope's arrival, the crowd cheered for many minutes, most craning to see the small figure of the Pope climb the stairway to join fifty bishops in the celebration of the mass. "Today, more than at any other time, we must have a priority of morality over technology," he said in his homily. "The same technology that has the possibility to help the poor sometimes even contributes to poverty."

WINNIPEG, MANITOBA, SUNDAY, SEPTEMBER 16

The theme of the Pope's visit to Winnipeg was "Faith and Culture in a Multicultural Society" and he responded by making an openly political speech endorsing minority-language rights and praising federalism. "In her own multicultural interaction, Canada not only offers to the world a creative vision of society, but she also has a splendid opportunity to show consistency between what she believes and what she does." His remarks were met with applause from the 150,000 gathered for the outdoor mass at Birds Hill Provincial Park where church officials had erected a dramatic eight-tiered, wood-and-steel altar adorned with more than 1,000 chrysanthemums.

Pope John Paul II celebrated the many cultures that make up Winnipeg by visiting Saints Vladimir and Olga Cathedral, headquarters of the Ukrainian Catholic Church in Canada, where he addressed 1,100 congregants in Ukrainian and blessed a statue of St. Vladmir.

He then travelled by Popemobile to St. Mary's Cathedral. The mass at Birds Hill Provincial Park was celebrated in nine languages; a 300-member choir sang in English, French and Ukrainian and the Credo was recited in Latin. The pontiff had visited the city in 1969 while still a cardinal.

EDMONTON, ALBERTA, MONDAY, SEPTEMBER 17

Pope John Paul II's visit is remembered for his emotional homily on Third World Poverty during an outdoor mass. His voice rising with anger and moral indignation, he warned that the "poor South will judge the rich North ... And the poor people and the poor nations poor in different ways, not only lacking food but also deprived of freedom and other human rights will judge those people who take these goods away from them, amassing to themselves the imperialistic monopoly of economic and political supremacy at the expense of others." He called for a "world where freedom is not an empty word and where the poor man Lazarus can sit down at the same table with the rich man."

For those who had spent the night at the Canadian Armed Forces base at Namao, just outside Edmonton, morning broke with the strains of *Ave Maria* followed by a recital by the Edmonton Symphony Orchestra and several local choirs. The Pope would celebrate the mass, which was attended by more than 150,000, from a three-tiered altar that soared above the crowd like a dove in flight and sparkled in the early morning sunshine. That afternoon, the pontiff, taking his first break in nine days, went walking among the wild buffalo at Elk Island National Park, east of Edmonton.

FORT SIMPSON/YELLOWKNIFE, NORTHWEST TERRITORIES, TUESDAY, SEPTEMBER 18

Despite their prayers, the fog did not lift and the Dene of Fort Simpson, in the Northwest Territories, were denied their audience with Pope John Paul II whose plane was forced to divert to Yellowknife. Hundreds of Dene had prepared for the visit, travelling for many miles across the high north in anticipation of the Pope's address. In Yellowknife, the Pope met with representatives of the Native Council of Canada, who were also fog-bound enroute to Fort Simpson. But the Holy Father — Yahitah as he is known to the Slavey Dene — promised the people of the tiny settlement, which sits within 500 kilometres of the Arctic Circle, he would return. Three years later, it was a promise kept.

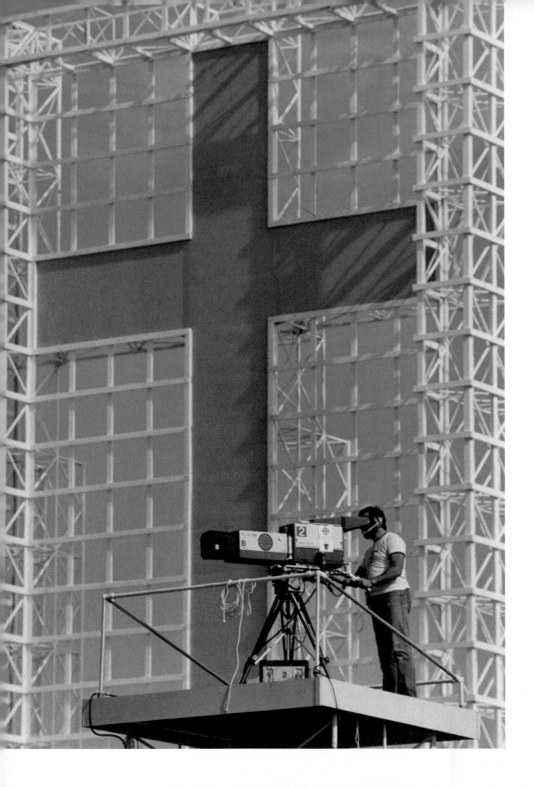

The boisterous welcome by more than 200,000 took the edge off the Pope's disappointment over missing his visit to the Dene of Fort Simpson. In contrast to Fort Simpson's fog, Abbotsford was bathed in brilliant sunshine and the crowd cheered and sang hymns as the Popemobile made its way through the grounds of the municipal airport — detouring several times so that everyone had a chance to greet the Holy Father before he celebrated mass.

Pope John Paul II was the first pope to visit the Pacific Coast of North America.

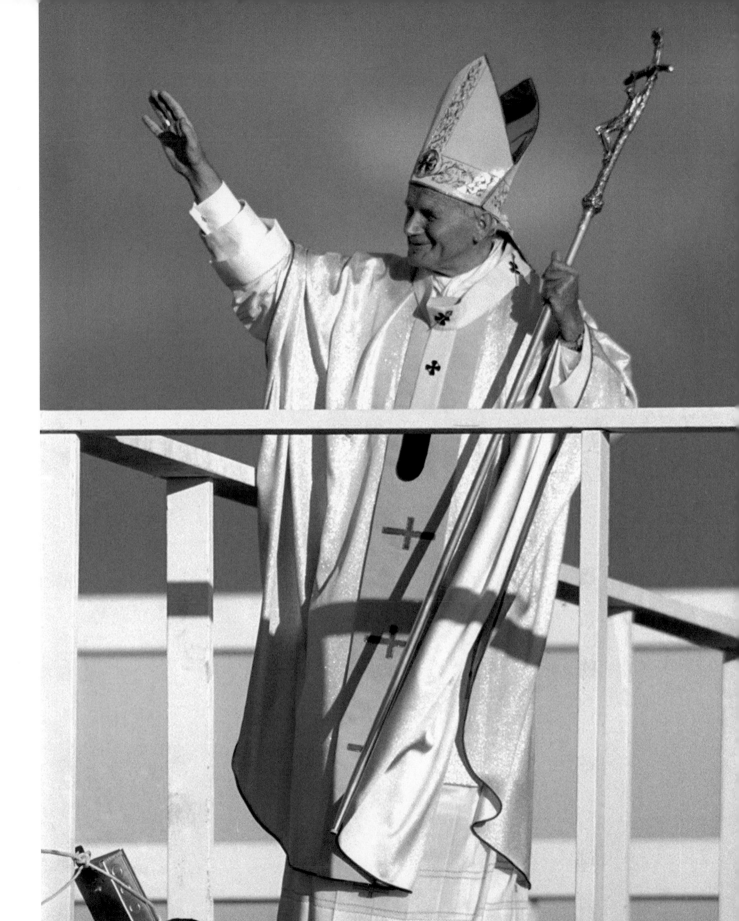

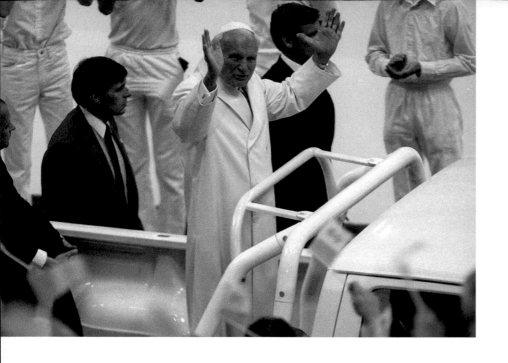

The crowd of mostly young people, the elderly and the disabled who attended the Pope's address at British Columbia's domed stadium provided the audience for his strongest condemnation of abortion of his Canadian tour and an impassioned opposition to artificial means of birth control.

> 66 In the plan of God, respect for the meaning of the body and for openness to life is a necessary condition for ensuring the full dignity of the human person, the full dignity of human life. 99
>
> — *Excerpt from the Pope's address at B.C. Place*

OTTAWA, ONTARIO, WEDNESDAY, SEPTEMBER 19

More than 250,000 people lined the Rideau Canal to see the Pope's flotilla — including the specially designed Popeboat — pass as classical music wafted from speakers. He waved and made the Sign of the Cross, blessing the thousands who had stood by the railings since early morning. He then boarded the Popemobile to drive through the streets of Hull where another 60,000 people lined that city's streets.

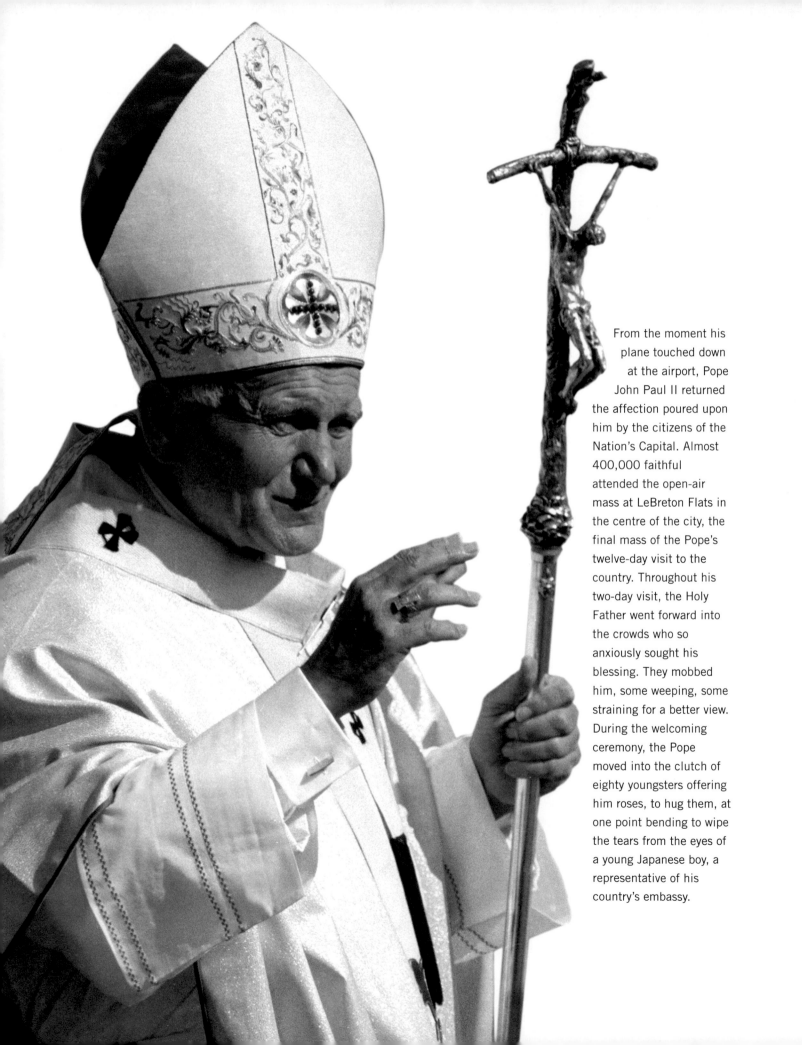

From the moment his plane touched down at the airport, Pope John Paul II returned the affection poured upon him by the citizens of the Nation's Capital. Almost 400,000 faithful attended the open-air mass at LeBreton Flats in the centre of the city, the final mass of the Pope's twelve-day visit to the country. Throughout his two-day visit, the Holy Father went forward into the crowds who so anxiously sought his blessing. They mobbed him, some weeping, some straining for a better view. During the welcoming ceremony, the Pope moved into the clutch of eighty youngsters offering him roses, to hug them, at one point bending to wipe the tears from the eyes of a young Japanese boy, a representative of his country's embassy.

CANADIAN FORCES BASE UPLANDS, OTTAWA, ONTARIO, THURSDAY, SEPTEMBER 20

"Goodbye, God bless you," was how Pope John Paul II bid farewell to Canadians during the official ceremonies at CFB Uplands attended by Governor-General Jeanne Sauvé and Prime Minister Brian Mulroney. The Pope expressed his "keen disappointment" that bad weather prevented a visit with the Dene at Fort Simpson but added, with a smile: "Excuse me — so I invited myself to the second time in Canada." A promise he would keep.

Fort Simpson, Northwest Territories ~ September 20,

1987

Three years after fog thwarted his planned visit to the

Dene settlement of Fort Simpson in 1984, Yahtitah, the

Father of Fathers, kept his promise to return, stopping at the end

of a ten-day tour of the United States. For a people who had seen

their share of broken promises, the Holy Father's five-hour

pilgrimage became a symbol of hope. The faith of the thousands

of pilgrims who streamed from across the North into the tiny

settlement was reinforced as a magnificent rainbow swept across

the northern horizon while Pope John Paul II once again

championed aboriginal rights.

A cold, steady drizzle and low-hanging clouds threatened in the early morning as more than 3,000 pilgrims took shelter in tents and under plastic sheets until a brilliant sun welcomed the pontiff's arrival. The site of the visit was a place the Dene, a group made up of the Dog-rib, Slavey, Chipewyan, Hareskin and Loucheux Indians of the Mackenzie Valley, consider an ancient, sacred meeting place.

❝ The soul of the native peoples of Canada is hungry for the spirit of God — because it is hungry for justice, peace, love, goodness, fortitude, responsibility and human dignity. This is a decisive time in your history… Be assured that the church will walk that path with you. **❞**

— Excerpt from Pope John Paul II's address to the pilgrims of Fort Simpson

A tent city was set up on the edge of town to accommodate the pilgrims who arrived as early as a week before the visit, swelling the town's population of 1,000 to nearly 3,000 by Sunday when the Pope arrived. Saturday evening, they fed the crowds with loaves and fishes — 2,000 fish to be exact, caught by eight local fishermen.

The Pope celebrated mass from an altar tucked inside a six-storey high, open-fronted white teepee. Aboriginal tribes from across the North were represented among the congregation: Métis, Inuit and the Dene. Reflecting this heritage, mass was celebrated in traditional Latin along with rhythmic, hypnotic drums and chanted hymns. The pontiff told the faithful that he came as a friend and, as had the missionaries who came before him, to proclaim God's word. He then made an appeal to the young people in the congregation to answer a calling and seek vocations in the priesthood and sisterhood.

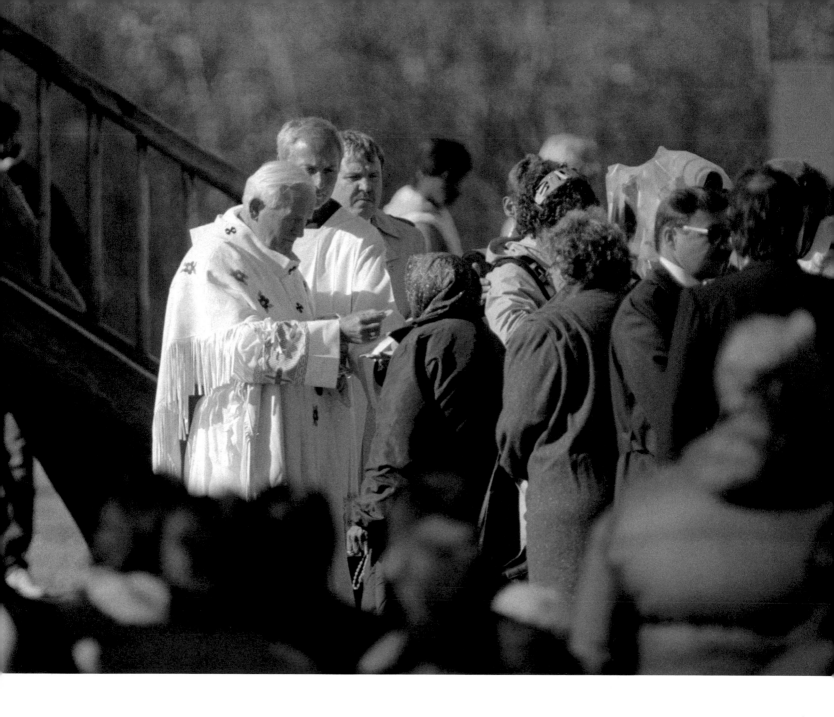

After reading the pontiff's prepared remarks, native leaders pleaded with him to re-affirm his call for aboriginal self-government and land claims. The Holy Father assured them that he had not backed away from his previous commitment, proclaimed in a radio message from Yellowknife in 1984, stating that he was on the record as supporting the aboriginal right to a "just and equitable measure of self-governing, along with a land base and adequate resources necessary for developing a viable economy."

For Canada's Aboriginal Peoples, the Pope's decision to return in 1987 was a milestone in the relationship between them and the Catholic Church, even though the pontiff failed to reiterate the acknowledgement he made in 1984 that the church and its clerics had made mistakes that they were at pains to repair. He had made a promise and he kept it.

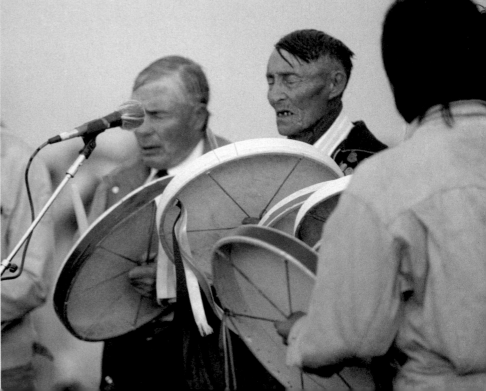

Toronto, Ontario ~ July 23-30,

2002

When Pope John Paul II arrived in July, 2002,
for what would be his last pilgrimage to Canada, he was frail and
hunched with age, trembling with Parkinson's, and yet his strength
and determination became a symbol to the hundreds of thousands of
young people who had congregated in Toronto to celebrate
World Youth Day. Throughout his seven-day stay, his sheer presence
overwhelmed those who lined the streets or crowded the fields
and halls, craning to see him. By the beginning of the new millennium,
Pope John Paul II had established himself as a man who had
shaped history and changed the world. In recognition, throughout this
final papal visit, the streets of Toronto resounded with the chant:
"John Paul Two, We Love You."

The Pope was welcomed at the airport by a gathering of young people and dignitaries, including Prime Minister Jean Chrétien. There had been concern that the ailing pontiff would be overcome by the schedule that lay ahead: A welcoming party at Toronto's Exhibition Stadium, a vigil at Downsview, the former Armed Forces base, followed by a mass there on Sunday morning. But he showed his strength that first day, surprising his entourage by descending from the plane with slow, laboured steps, ignoring the hydraulic lift offered him.

The city vibrated with the passion of the young who swarmed the streets, bearing the flags of their countries, carrying crucifixes and papal banners. Small groups broke into song on street corners. The field at Downsview, where 800,000 — more than double the crowd organizers anticipated — would celebrate the final mass, became a shanty town of tiny tents and cardboard-box lean-tos, shelters against the unyielding heat and cloying humidity. On the eve of the mass, a rainstorm swept through but failed to dampen the spirits of the enormous crowd, who chanted and sang once the Pope arrived.

Riding on the enthusiasm of nearly one million young people from every continent on Earth, the week was a festival of Roman Catholic faith. John Paul had created World Youth Day in 1985 — the centrepiece of which is a triduum, a three-day celebration of liturgy culminating in an outdoor mass — to bring together young Catholics from across the world. When he chose Toronto as the host of the celebration for 2002, he proclaimed: "Come and make the great avenues of Toronto resound with the joyful tidings that Christ loves every person and brings to fulfillment every trace of goodness, beauty and truth found in the city of man."

Before Sunday's mass, more than 300,000 young Catholics trekked several kilometres through the streets of Toronto, — singing and praying their devotion — before arriving at Downsview where they would sit in all-night vigil traditionally associated with Christ's vigil before His crucifixion.

The rain swept through Downsview in the early morning, ending just as the Holy Father and the 400 bishops and 1,000 priests were climbing the altar to begin mass. In his homily, the Pope confronted the sex-scandals involving Catholic clergy in North America: "Do not be discouraged by the sins and failings of some (Church) members.
The harm done by some priests and religious to the young and vulnerable fills us all with a deep sense of sadness and shame. But think of the vast majority of dedicated and generous priests whose only wish is to serve and do good."

Pope John Paul II left Canada for the final time as he had arrived nearly twenty years before, a symbol of strength, joy and faith. Once again, he ignored the hydraulic lift readied to lift him to the airplane waiting to fly him to Mexico and Guatemala. Instead, he slowly mounted the steep staircase, bent and hurting but determined. He had touched hundreds of thousands of young people who had experienced their faith as they had never done before — and may never again. He filled them with joy and profound emotion. "You are young," he told them, "and the Pope is old, and a bit tired. But he still fully identifies with your hopes and aspirations ... no difficulty, no fear is so great that it can suffocate the hope that springs eternal in the hearts of the young."

As he left, the anthem of World Youth Day echoed in the hearts of all Canadians:

"Light of the world.
Salt of the earth.
Be for the world the
* face of love*
Be for the earth the
* reflection of His light."*

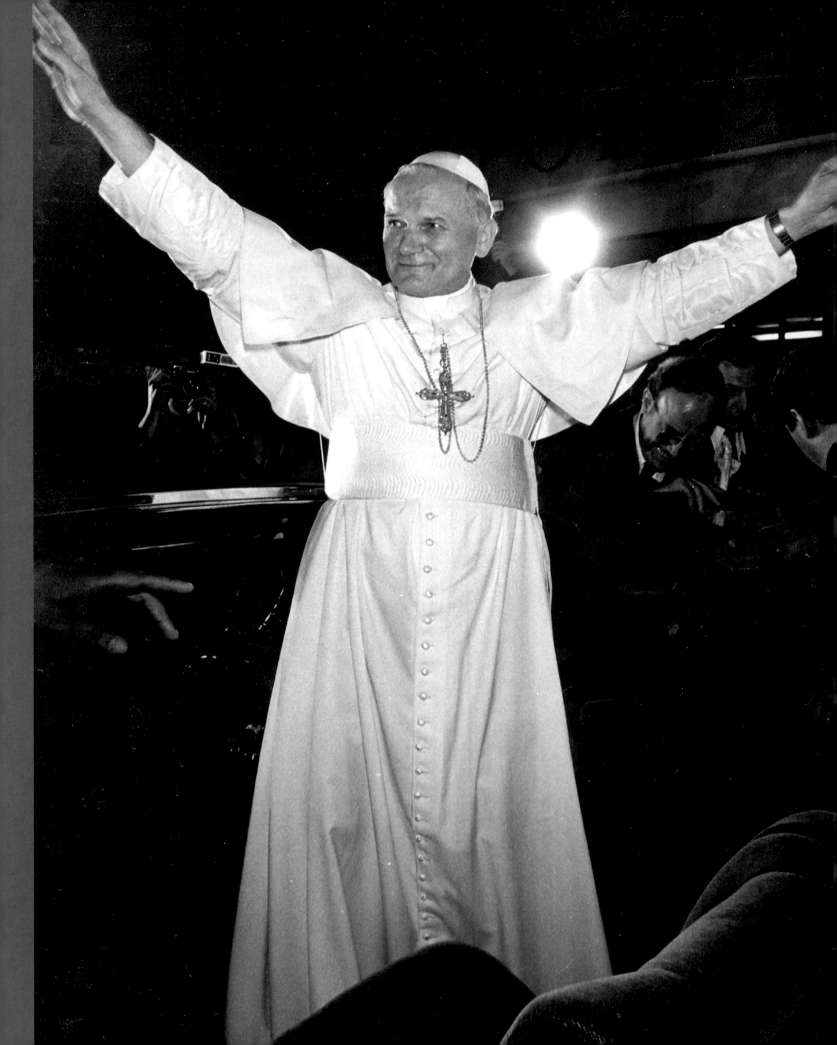

THE FATHER WHO CHANGED HISTORY

John Paul, the pope who shook communism to its foundations,
affected the lives of billions of people across the world
with his spiritual luminosity, compassion and moral firmness.

BY CHARLES ENMAN

WITH THE DEATH OF JOHN PAUL II, THE 264TH HOLY FATHER OF THE WORLD'S BILLION Roman Catholics is gone — but so, too, is a man whose charisma and moral authority changed history for Catholic and non-Catholic alike.

Many considered him among the most influential popes of the last four centuries. Certainly, no pope has touched as many human beings as John Paul did on the more than one hundred pastoral visits and pilgrimages he made across the world.

Opinion on his legacy is divided among his own flock. The Roman Catholic Church was at a crossroads when John Paul assumed the papacy. Calls for modernization, for "relevance," were heard from many corners. Equally strong were protests that long-established positions on morality, on the sanctity of life, on sexual matters, must be upheld. God himself surely did not sway with current fashion.

Wherever he spoke, this man of unending prayer reached out with a moral authority rare in modern times.

During the late 1970s, this first-ever Polish pope so charged his fellow Poles with visions of freedom and justice that the Communist regime was shaken to its foundations, beginning a political self-affirmation that a decade later swept away the Marxist regimes of Eastern Europe.

Mikhail Gorbachev, who presided over the Soviet Union's dissolution, would later write: "One can say that everything that has happened in Eastern Europe in recent years would have been impossible without the pope's efforts and the enormous role, including the political role, he has played in the world arena."

(Opposite) Pope John Paul II seen in 1978 a few days after his election as Pope

John Paul's moral authority was no less obvious when, on the first official papal visit to the Holy Land in March 2000, he appealed to Christians, Jews, and Muslims — "the children of Abraham," he called them — to affirm their spiritual commonality. During those memorable six days, as he addressed thousands — Christians, Jews and Muslims alike — this ailing man called for "a new era of peace and understanding in the Holy Land."

Palestinians heard him affirm the justice of their collective aspirations. "Your torment is before the eyes of the world, and it has gone on too long," the pontiff told them. "The Palestinian people have the natural right to a homeland and the right to be able to live in peace and security with the other peoples of this area."

But John Paul was no less sensitive to the historical grievances of the world's Jews. "I assure the Jewish people that the Catholic Church is deeply saddened by the hatred, acts of persecution, and displays of anti-Semitism directed against the Jews by Christians at any time and in any place," a tearful John Paul declared in the crowded Yad Vashem memorial centre on a hill above Jerusalem.

Another of his memorable journeys was his visit to Cuba in January 1998. He never once mentioned the Castro regime but denounced Cuba's political system as withering to the dignity of the human person. (In fairness, he also deplored the American economic embargo.)

Nearly four decades after the Cuban Revolution, Cuban crowds chanted, "*Libertad, libertad.*" At an address at Camaguey, 200,000 teenagers cheered him wildly; none of them had ever lived under a regime that encouraged religious practice.

The largest gathering in history — five million to seven million people — came to hear him speak on World Youth Day in Manila in 1995. There, he rebuked the hedonism and the materialism of the Western Hemisphere, deploring all slavery to "false and superficial gratifications."

The church under John Paul strengthened its opposition to abortion, infanticide, euthanasia, and capital punishment. He resolutely opposed birth control, divorce and remarriage, married priests, and the ordination of woman.

"I am not severe — I am sweet by nature," the Pope once said. "But I defend the rigidity principle. God is stronger than human weakness and deviations. God will always have the last word."

AFTER POPE PAUL VI DIED IN AUGUST 1978, IT FELL TO THE CARDINALS OF THE ROMAN CATHOLIC church to elect a new pope. On August 26, they elected Albino Cardinal Luciani, archbishop of Venice, whose reign as John Paul I ended with his sudden death only thirty-three days after his election.

At the second conclave, assembled in Rome in October, the 111 cardinals considered the possibility of choosing someone from outside Italy to lead the church for the first time in 455 years. In the wake of the Second Vatican Council, which was held from 1962-65, the entire structure of the church had been re-organized, a difficult process still under way that required a pope with experience in running parishes, dioceses, and archdioceses. In short, a "pastoral" pope was needed.

This seemed to point in the direction of the obscure Karol Jósef Cardinal Wojtyla of Krakow. As Enrique y Cardinal Tarancón, the archbishop of Madrid said, "We wanted a pastor more than an intellectual, and with his Polish pastoral experience, his pastoral way of being, his direct contact with the masses, Wojtyla was the man we had sought. It was very healthy psychologically for the church to have a humanist as pope, someone close to the people."

Ideally, the new pope would also be young enough to lead the church into the Third Millennium. At fifty-eight, the robustly healthy Wojtyla not only suited, but was, in some eyes, still on the young side.

On October 16, 1978, in the final round of voting, Wojtyla had ninety-four of 111 votes. Asked if he would accept, he was forthright. "It is God's will," he said. "I accept," becoming the youngest pope in 122 years.

The crowd's response was muted when the name of the new pope was announced on St. Peter's Square. No one knew his name. Some, among the vastly Italian crowd, believed that this unfamiliar name "Wojtyla" must be African. No one then could have had any notion of how profoundly he was to mark his church and his world.

KAROL JÓSEF WOJTYLA WAS BORN MAY 18, 1920, IN THE SOUTHERN POLISH TOWN OF Wadowice. His father was a retired army officer, deeply patriotic and religious. The man who, as pope, often spoke of the spiritual uses of suffering, had lived through personal tragedy from childhood. His entire family died before he was twenty-two. A sister died in infancy. At eight, he lost his mother; at eleven, his older brother; and just before his twenty-second birthday, his beloved father died.

Karol Wojtyla was an extraordinary student, always leading his classes. Not merely bookish, he was popular in every circle he frequented. From early in life, he was devoted to the Virgin Mary. He believed, in his final decades, that Mary had saved his life several times and taught him how to suffer. When he spent May 1994, in hospital, recovering from a broken hip, he said, "Through Mary, I would like to express my gratitude again today for this gift of suffering."

Wojtyla was a natural actor, a gift that would serve him well on the world's stage. He was also a bit of a daredevil in his youth who loved to ski, kayak and play soccer. He skied until his mid-70s, when a fragile hip ended the hobby.

From childhood, Wojtyla loved to go to Kalwaria Zebrzybowska, a Bernardine fathers' monastery fifty kilometres from his hometown. There, each Easter, tens of thousands of rural inhabitants gathered to witness a re-enactment of the Passion and Resurrection of Christ.

Wojtyla never made a display of religious belief, but he was always given over to prayer and meditation. His concentration was so deep that he seemed to retreat from his immediate surroundings. Even in frail old age, prayer and meditation could invigorate his eyes and his smile.

Many Jews lived in Wadowice, and Wojtyla was always aware of his commonality with them. His family was one of the few that evinced no signs of anti-Semitism. Young Karol became upset when a young Jewish girl, Ginka Beer, who lived in the same apartment building, told him her family was leaving for Palestine to escape prejudice.

Fifty years later, Ginka, now Regina Reisenfeld, attended a general audience on St. Peter's Square. Wojtyla, now Pope John Paul, recognized her. He was deeply moved at news that her mother had died in a death camp, and her father in the Soviet Union.

"He just looked at me, and there was deep compassion in his eyes," she recalled. "He took both my hands and for almost two minutes he blessed me and prayed before me, just holding my hands in his hands. There were thousands of people in the square, but for just a few seconds there were just the two of us."

During the German occupation of Poland, Wojtyla worked in a quarry. He never forgot the connection he had forged with peasants and workers. He was also a member of the Polish underground and a clandestine student at a seminary.

He spoke six languages besides his native Polish, with Italian, Spanish, German and French being the best.

In November 1946, he was ordained a priest. He earned his first doctorate, in mystical theology, at twenty-eight, and his second, in philosophy, at thirty-three. In 1954, he was appointed professor of Christian Philosophy at the Catholic University in Lublin, the only Catholic university behind the Iron Curtain. From there, his rise through church ranks was rapid. In December 1963, he was appointed archbishop of Krakow.

The Second Vatican Council had begun meeting in Rome the year before, and Wojtyla had attended with the other Polish bishops. He believed that council could do no better than to affirm the transcendence of the human person against materialism, themes that resonated in him for the remainder of his life.

He was not comfortable with the more harsh critiques that his fellow bishops made against the church hierarchy. Nonetheless, he joined in votes that called for extensive reform of the church, especially a reduction of the power of the Curia, the central administrative body.

Years later, he described the Second Vatican Council as "nothing less than a Magna Carta, a great charter designed to make the church available for the preaching of the Gospel in the world of today."

In 1967, he was named cardinal archbishop of Krakow, becoming, at forty-seven, one of the church's youngest cardinals. Even the UB, the Polish secret police, run by the Soviets, were impressed by the newly appointed cardinal. In a document written only five weeks after he became a cardinal, the UB described this new and obviously significant opponent of the regime. "He deftly reconciles traditional popular religiosity with intellectual Catholicism ... "

PAPAL VISITS TO FOREIGN LANDS WERE RARE BEFORE HIS PAPACY. BUT IN 1979, JOHN PAUL II journeyed to Mexico, Poland, Ireland, the United States, and Turkey. When he descended from his plane in Mexico City, he was mobbed. In six days, John Paul gave twenty-six speeches and homilies. He met with church people, peasants, natives, students, slum dwellers. No such broad encounter between a pope and a people had been seen before.

The Mexican visit set the pattern for his future tours. Everywhere, he would evoke the personal nature of the believer's encounter with God.

On June 2, 1979, John Paul began his first official visit to Poland, his homeland. The reception there was even more rapturous. Crowds millions-strong gathered to hear him. "We want God. We want God," they chanted.

The adulation was so unanimous that the Communist regime could only watch. By the end of his visit, all pretensions that the Communist Party spoke for the people had become risible. Only months later, Solidarity, the political movement that won Poles their freedom, would be born.

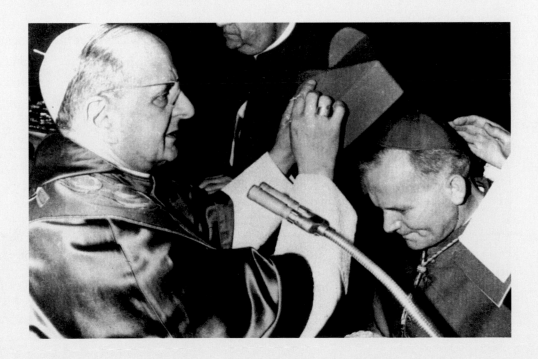

Pope Paul VI places the cardinal's hat on the head of Karol Wojtyla in 1967, declaring him a cardinal.

In the opening years of his papacy, John Paul seemed to move from triumph to triumph. But on May 13, 1981, in St. Peter's Square, he was shot by Mehmet Ali Agca, a Turkish terrorist, whose bullets wounded him in the stomach, the right elbow, and a finger. He lost sixty per cent of his blood and was given the Anointing of the Sick, sometimes referred to as last rites. Miraculously, as the Pope put it, no vital organ had been hit, although surgeons removed a section of his intestine.

The assumption has emerged that Mehmet Ali Agca had acted as an agent for the Bulgarian secret service, itself controlled by the Soviet KGB. But no one really knows.

John Paul visited Mr. Agca in prison and spoke with him for twenty minutes. At the end, the prisoner kissed the pope's hand. Later, he would say that "the pope knows everything." (The would-be assassin's attitude hardened after his pardon in 2000, when he described the pope as "the incarnation of all that is capitalism.")

EVEN AT THE VERY END OF HIS LIFE, WEAKENED BY PARKINSON'S, JOHN PAUL RETAINED HIS resolve to promote Christian values to a recalcitrant world. He staunchly opposed the second Iraq war, sending envoys to Baghdad and Washington to plead for peace.

There has been no global exodus from the Catholic Church during John Paul's papacy. When he first sat on St. Peter's Throne, there were some 700 million professing Catholics. Today, there are more than one billion.

In his declining years, his moral authority seemed to grow for the world at large, a legacy, perhaps, of his evident acceptance of his own suffering. Some observers believe he may one day be called John Paul the Great, like Leo the Great and Gregory the Great.

His luminosity of spirit, his compassion and his moral firmness were evident even to many who had never graced the doorway of a Catholic church. No pontiff in centuries has equaled his influence on the political scene. His human stature seemed beyond cavil anywhere in the temporal world he served with such zealous spiritual devotion.

Sources: *Witness to Hope: The Biography of John Paul II*, by George Weigel; *Pope John Paul II: The Biography*, by Tad Szulc; *His Holiness: John Paul II and the Hidden History of Our Time*, by Carl Bernstein and Marco Politi; *Christian History* magazine, *National Catholic Reporter*, *Time* magazine, *Newsweek* magazine.

ACKNOWLEDGEMENTS

Appreciation and admiration go to the more than fifty journalists whose stories and
photographs — pulled from the CanWest archives — are the bedrock of this book.
As Pastor and Brother reflects their talents and commitment to their craft.
Thanks must also go to the various photo editors, photo technicians (especially Scott Parker
and Howard Fagen at the *Ottawa Citizen*) and librarians at newspapers across CanWest
who were so generous with their time and patience.

— *Lynn McAuley*

The publisher gratefully acknowledges permission to reproduce the following
material in this book. Every reasonable effort has been made to contact the copyright holders;
in the event of an inadvertent omission or error, please notify the publisher.

Photographs in this book were reprinted with the permission of the following newspapers:

The National Post
The Windsor Star
The Montreal Gazette
The Ottawa Citizen
The Calgary Herald
The Edmonton Journal
The Vancouver Province
The Vancouver Sun

Photographers whose work appears throughout *As Pastor and Brother* are:

Richard Arless, Jr.
Doug Ball
Lynn Ball
Gordon Beck
George Bird
Chris Bolin
Nick Brancaccio
Peter Brousseau
Tedd Church
George Cree
Wayne Cuddington
Michael Dugas
Gerry Kahrmann
Jean Levac

John Mahoney
Steve Makris
Tim McKenna
Randy Moore
Pierre Obendrauf
Bruno Schlumberger
Chris Schwarz
Len Sidaway
Ray Smith

Cover photo:
CP (Plinio Lepri)

Page 77, Pope at Elk Island:
CP (Arturo Mari)

Page 107: Reuters
(Gabriel Bouys)

Page 108, top:
CP (Kevin Frayer)

Page 117, bottom right:
CP (Kevin Frayer)

Page 120: Reuters
(Mal Langsdon)

Page 125: CP

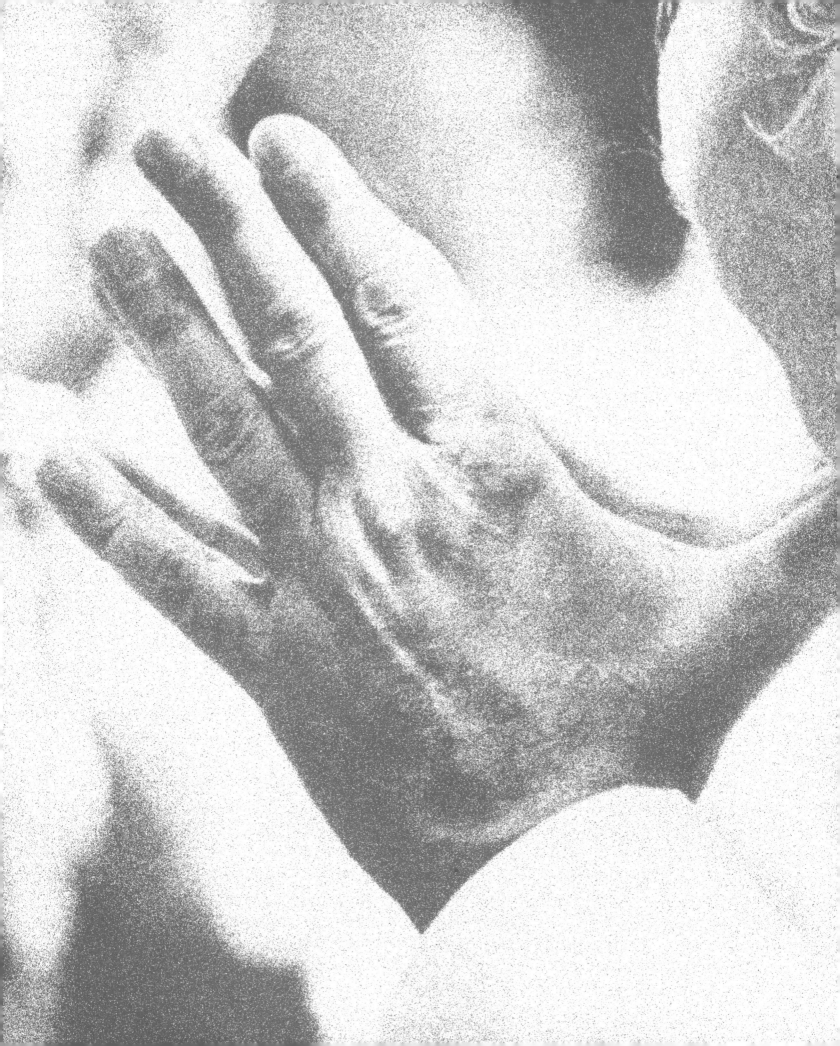